Getting the Most from Pairwise Testing

A Guide for Practicing Software Engineers

George B. Sherwood
Testcover.com, LLC

Contents

Introduction

Pairwise (or all-pairs) testing is a powerful technique for generating test configurations and test data. These designs produce small sets of test cases that cover all pairs of test interactions. Compared with random selection of test parameters, pairwise designs provide comparable coverage with far fewer test cases. Thus, pairwise designs can lead to more effective testing, for improved quality and cost savings.

The purpose of this guide is to provide practicing software engineers with a concise summary of the technique. Several examples are provided to illustrate designs for configurations, input values, database tables and state model transitions. These are meant to be a quick reference for how similar problems can be analyzed and what considerations go into an effective test design. Collectively, the examples support 3 main points as follows.

> **Versatility** – Pairwise testing is versatile as well as powerful. The diverse examples described in the guide – physical configurations, HTML form inputs, database records and state model transitions – demonstrate general pairwise design principles. These principles can be applied to a broad range of test situations extending pairwise testing benefits beyond the sample provided here.
>
> **Handling real-world constraints** – Several examples show the need to conform to real-world constraints of the system under test: Certain combinations of test factors may be unsupported or may not lead to an expected test result. However, beyond the recognition of this need are the illustrations of meeting it in everyday test designs. The constraints may be complex, depending on 3 or more test factors,

but they can be handled easily in pairwise designs.

Attention to system behavior – An important theme throughout the guide is that pairwise designs can, and need to, reflect an appropriate attention to system behavior. Selection of input data must exercise the states of the system as defined by its specification or model. The guide aims to demonstrate, with the examples, that test plans to verify required system behavior are not just feasible. They are practical outcomes of pairwise test design.

Additional material in the guide addresses the basis for pairwise testing, its relation to higher-strength designs, and considerations for selecting a pairwise test tool. An appendix provides the test case generator input for all of the examples. Thus, interested readers can examine the design techniques in more detail and verify the results.

Generally this material is intended to be accessible to software practitioners, without a need for external references. However readers who are unfamiliar with the test design concepts of *equivalence partitioning* and *boundary value analysis* can find descriptions in Wikipedia and other online sources. *State model* descriptions are also available online. Additional detail on topics in the guide can be found at Testcover.com as well.

Basis for pairwise test designs

Pairwise testing aims to use the minimum number of test cases. A small number is important for specifying configurations, which may be costly to acquire and set up. Similarly, a small number of functional tests limits execution time and cost. It does not matter whether the tests are performed manually or with automation – Fewer tests take less time to run.

Pairwise testing uses ideas from the design of experiments, which includes techniques broadly applied to scientific research, clinical trials, opinion polls and more. Pairwise testing has characteristics which make it very efficient for testing complex systems of software and hardware. Understanding these characteristics is important for employing the technique where it is suitable, and for having appropriate expectations of its benefits. Minimizing the number of test cases leads to the following characteristics of pairwise testing.

> **Pass/fail results** – Pairwise tests have results that pass or fail. A test case can answer the question, "Does the expected response return in less than 5 seconds?" It does not answer the question, "What is the average response time at a particular system load?"
>
> **Deterministic results** – When a pairwise test case returns the expected result once, it passes. There is nothing built into the design to try again, to account for uncontrolled variables. In a complex system, testing one area may depend on other uncontrolled parts of the system working correctly. Often this dependency is not an issue for verifying correct operation of the system. However, pairwise testing, as described here, does not address the question, "What percent of test attempts get the correct result?" Additional test cases would be required.

In sum, pairwise testing offers test designs with relatively few test cases, but the technique is not intended to answer all possible questions. Consequently it has an important place, with other complementary techniques, in the software engineer's toolbox.

Pairwise designs for configurations

Pairwise designs for configurations of hardware and software include all allowed pairs of values using a relatively small number of configurations. Two designs are illustrated here. In the first example all pairs of values are allowed. I.e. there are no constraints. The second example shows how unsupported or impossible combinations can be avoided.

Configurations without constraints

In this example there are three new applications to be tested on a networked computer. We need to specify which test configurations will be used to run a suite of system tests. We have determined that there are four test factors to be varied during the tests – the operating system, the network connection type, the browser, and the application. The table shows the required values.

Configuration values without constraints			
Test factor	**Values**		
Op system	XP	Vista	Win7
Connection	wi-fi	dsl	cable
Browser	IE	Firefox	Safari
Application	App1	App2	App3

Because we have 4 factors with 3 values, there are 3 x 3 x 3 x 3 = 81 possible configurations. We don't have the time or the resources for 81 configurations. It is not practical to test all of them.

In this example there is an orthogonal array which can be used as a template for the configurations. The array has 4 columns corresponding to the 4 test factors. Each column has 3 values which represent the 3 values of the corresponding test factor. The array gives 9 configurations as follows.

Configurations without constraints			
Op system	**Connection**	**Browser**	**Application**
XP	wi-fi	IE	App1
XP	dsl	Firefox	App2
XP	cable	Safari	App3
Vista	wi-fi	Firefox	App3
Vista	dsl	Safari	App1
Vista	cable	IE	App2
Win7	wi-fi	Safari	App2
Win7	dsl	IE	App3
Win7	cable	Firefox	App1

Examination of the configurations shows that each value of any test factor is paired with all the values of the other factors. E.g. XP is paired with all values of the other factors in the first 3 configurations. In total, there are 54 pairs covered in the 9 configurations. Each configuration includes 6 pairs, and none of them is repeated.

It is possible to use an orthogonal array here because all pairs of factor values are allowed. However, when there are combinations of values to exclude, as in the next example, a different method is needed to generate the test cases.

Configurations with constraints

The second example is similar to the first but with different operating system values. The table shows the required values.

Configuration values with constraints			
Test factor	**Values**		
Op system	XP	MacOS	Linux
Connection	wi-fi	dsl	cable
Browser	IE	Firefox	Safari
Application	App1	App2	App3

The orthogonal array we used in the first example paired the Internet Explorer (IE) browser with all three operating systems. But the only pair that is supported and represents a valid configuration in the second example is Windows XP with IE. And although Firefox is supported with all three operating systems, Safari is supported only on XP and MacOS. If we try to use the orthogonal array from the first example here, three configurations will be unsupported, as follows.

Unsupported configurations			
Op system	**Connection**	**Browser**	**Application**
MacOS	cable	IE	App2
Linux	dsl	IE	App3
Linux	wi-fi	Safari	App2

Removing these configurations from the plan does not solve the problem because that would remove coverage of pairs which *are* allowed (IE with App2, Safari with wi-fi, etc.). Thus a different method is needed to generate the test cases, one that is more general and can accommodate constraints. Typically an automated search is used to generate the test cases. Compared with selecting arrays manually, automated searches are usually faster and more accurate.

To finish this example, the following table gives a set of configurations which covers all 51 of the allowed pairs, but not the 3 unsupported ones.

Configuration values with constraints			
Op system	**Connection**	**Browser**	**Application**
XP	wi-fi	Firefox	App1
MacOS	dsl	Firefox	App2
Linux	cable	Firefox	App3
MacOS	cable	Safari	App1
XP	dsl	Safari	App3
XP	cable	IE	App2
MacOS	wi-fi	Safari	App3
Linux	wi-fi	Firefox	App2
Linux	dsl	Firefox	App1
XP	dsl	IE	App3
XP	wi-fi	IE	App1
XP	wi-fi	Safari	App2

Pairwise designs for input values

Pairwise testing also can be effective for selecting combinations of input values. Pairwise designs can cover the allowed pairs of values using far fewer test cases than with random selection. Thus better test coverage can be achieved with fewer test cases.

A typical pairwise input value illustration follows.

> "There is a system with **k** inputs, and each input can take one of **v** values. Even if **v** is a small number, for a realistically large number of inputs **k**, it is impossible for anyone to test all $\mathbf{v}^{\mathbf{k}}$ combinations before the sun burns up its helium. On the other hand, with a pairwise

> design there are only about $\mathbf{v}^2$ test cases. So the results of the first pass can be ready Tuesday. And importantly, the design has better coverage than a comparable number of random test cases."

The illustration is all right as far as it goes, but it glosses over the fact that the system has **s** states which respond differently to inputs. The state of the system must be controlled to know what actually is being tested. The test design depends on a specification or model of how the system is *supposed* to work, so the system states, their set-up steps, and input responses can be examined. It is not enough to select $\mathbf{v}^2$ pairwise cases without considering system behavior.

Partitions for expected results

Generally, testing multiple states requires partitioning the input values so that each partition leads to a different expected result (state). We find the appropriate equivalence classes and boundary values of input data for each expected result. Then we can generate the test cases for all pairs of input values in the partition.

For example, in a design-your-burger application using an HTML form, there are several types of inputs: a menu, a radio button, 8 checkboxes, buttons to reset or submit the form and links to other pages. We want to test the action of the form with all pairs of input values.

To start we could associate each input with a test factor, as in the table below. (Here 'none' means no input value provided.)

Design-your-burger form inputs					
Name	**Type**	**Values**			
Burger	menu	beef	turkey	veggie	
Cooked	radio	none	rare	medium	well
Cheese	checkbox	no	yes		
Lettuce	checkbox	no	yes		
Tomato	checkbox	no	yes		
Onion	checkbox	no	yes		
Ketchup	checkbox	no	yes		
Mustard	checkbox	no	yes		
Mayo	checkbox	no	yes		
Secret sauce	checkbox	no	yes		
Reset	reset	none	reset		
Submit	submit	none	submit		
Nutrition facts	link	none	click		
About the chef	link	none	click		

Examination of these inputs shows that the reset, submit and link inputs are different from the others. They change the state, and they do so in different ways. The submit button is the trigger to start the processing of the form's data. The reset button clears the form, and the links go to other pages entirely.

In this partition we want to test that the submit button and the resulting processing work correctly. Inputs from the reset button and the links should not be included in the partition because they do not lead to the expected result state. If all the inputs *are* mixed into the same partition, we can expect some input value pairs will never test the action of the form – They simply will be reset or lost on the way to other pages.

The 10 test factors chosen in this example are the menu, radio button and 8 checkboxes. The test cases give the corresponding values in the table on the next page. Each pair of input values is included in at least one test case. In this partition, the submit button is clicked after the input values are set. The reset button and links to other pages are not used in these test cases.

Design-your-burger form inputs using submit button

Burger	Cooked	Cheese	Lettuce	Tomato	Onion	Ketchup	Mustard	Mayo	Secret sauce
turkey	well	yes	yes	no	yes	no	no	no	yes
veggie	none	yes	no	yes	no	yes	yes	yes	no
beef	rare	no	yes	no	yes	yes	no	yes	no
turkey	medium	no	no	yes	yes	yes	yes	yes	yes
beef	none	no	no	no	no	no	no	no	yes
veggie	rare	yes	no	yes	no	no	yes	no	yes
veggie	medium	yes	yes	no	no	no	no	yes	no
beef	well	no	no	yes	no	yes	yes	yes	yes
turkey	rare	no	yes	yes	no	yes	no	no	no
turkey	none	yes	yes	no	yes	no	yes	no	no
veggie	well	no	yes	no	yes	yes	no	yes	no
beef	medium	yes	yes	yes	yes	no	no	no	yes

Partitions for error results

In the design-your-burger example we used a partition for a normal result. The design of the interface did not allow input with errors. However, if the action of an HTML form detects and processes input errors, these erroneous values (or combinations of values) need to be excluded from the partition(s) for normal results. The situation is similar to including the reset button earlier. Erroneous values do not lead to normal results. So pairs that need to be tested in normal processing may not be tested if error values are mixed in. Of course, error values can be included in separate partitions for error processing states, as needed.

Pairwise designs for input values need constraints sometimes to insure that the combinations of values in a partition lead to the same expected result. For example if an HTML form takes months and days as inputs, day 31 should give a normal result only for the long months, January, March, May, etc. If April 31 is a possible input, it should lead to an error result in a different partition instead.

In summary, pairwise designs for input values need separate partitions to associate combinations of values with different expected results. The constrained factor values in each partition can be thought of as the degrees of freedom between the initial state set up and the results state expected. The pairwise tests exercise all pairs of values contained in the partition.

Pairwise designs for databases

Pairwise designs also can be used to select values in test database records. Production database dumps, scrubbed for privacy, are useful for testing of course. However, when new features are developed, test databases need to contain records which will exercise functions of the new features. The following example shows a pairwise design for testing a motel reservation system. In this example constraints are used to conform to the motel chain's business rules.

The motel chain is implementing an expansion program, building three new motels with innovative features and amenities. The company also is updating its reservation system to reflect these improvements. The software engineers working on the reservation system have migrated the old database to the new system for testing. However they need additional data to represent the motels under construction and their new features. The motel room database table has columns (factors) as follows.

Reservation database values			
Column	**Values**		
Location ID	[unique motel identifier]		
Room ID	[unique room identifier]		
Room type	single	standard	suite
Section	floor_1	mezzanine	tower
Smoking	no	yes	
Beds	single	2_queen	1_king
Convertible couch	no	yes	
Near gym/spa	no	yes	
Near business center	no	yes	
Wi-fi	no	yes	
Phone lines	1	2	
Balcony/patio	no	yes	

The engineers will use three Location ID values to represent the new motels. They will generate rows of data including all pairs of values for all the columns except the Room ID. (Each Room ID value should appear only once in the table.) The engineers will assign a single value as a Room ID placeholder to generate the rows. Then they will assign unique values to the Room IDs in the resulting rows (test records).

Business rule constraints

The three Room types define the allowed values for the other columns as follows.

- Each **single** room is located on floor_1 or in the tower in any of the new motels. Smoking may or may not be allowed. The single room has a single bed and does not have a convertible couch. It is not near a gym/spa or a business center. The room does not have wi-fi, but it does have 1 phone line. It does not have a balcony/patio.
- Each **standard** room is located in any section of any of the new motels. Smoking may or may not be allowed. The standard room has either 2 queen size beds or 1 king size bed. It does not have a convertible couch. The standard room may or may not be near a gym/spa or a business center. The room may or may not have wi-fi, and it does have 1 phone line. The standard room may or may not have a balcony/patio.
- Each **suite** is located in the mezzanine or tower of any of the new motels. Smoking may or may not be allowed. The suite has 2 queen size beds and a convertible couch. The suite is near a gym/spa and a business center. It has wi-fi and 2 phone lines. The suite also has a balcony/patio.

The following 15 records contain all allowed pairs of values consistent with the motel chain's business rules. The engineers will add these records to the motel room table for testing.

Reservation database records

Location ID	Room ID	Room type	Section	Smoking	Beds	Convertible couch	Near gym/spa	Near business center	Wi-fi	Phone lines	Balcony/patio
location_1	room_1	single	floor_1	no	single	no	no	no	no	1	no
location_2	room_2	suite	mezzanine	yes	2_queen	yes	yes	yes	yes	2	yes
location_3	room_3	standard	tower	no	1_king	no	no	yes	yes	1	yes
location_3	room_4	standard	floor_1	yes	1_king	no	yes	no	no	1	no
location_2	room_5	standard	tower	no	2_queen	no	no	no	no	1	no
location_1	room_6	standard	mezzanine	no	1_king	no	yes	no	no	1	yes
location_1	room_7	suite	tower	yes	2_queen	yes	yes	yes	yes	2	yes
location_3	room_8	suite	tower	no	2_queen	yes	yes	yes	yes	2	yes
location_2	room_9	single	floor_1	yes	single	no	no	no	no	1	no
location_3	room_10	single	tower	no	single	no	no	no	no	1	no
location_3	room_11	standard	mezzanine	no	2_queen	no	yes	no	yes	1	no
location_2	room_12	standard	floor_1	no	1_king	no	yes	yes	no	1	yes
location_1	room_13	standard	floor_1	yes	2_queen	no	no	yes	yes	1	yes
location_1	room_14	standard	tower	yes	2_queen	no	yes	yes	yes	1	no
location_2	room_15	standard	mezzanine	yes	2_queen	no	no	yes	yes	1	yes

Pairwise designs for state models

Software engineers who use state models to describe the behavior of systems can use pairwise designs to test them. Testing a state transition consists of setting up the source or "from" state, triggering the transition and observing the results. The expectation is that the target or "to" state indicated by the model will result. Complex systems often use multiple state models working in parallel to describe overall behavior. The concurrent models are called orthogonal regions, and the overall system is described by the states of all the regions.

Test factors for a state model (one region) include the current from state, associated program variables and the state transition trigger event. The states of other regions may be test factors also, depending on the scope of the testing.

Here again, pairwise designs can provide a limited number of test cases to exercise the system using all pairs of test values according to the state model.

2-state example

This example uses a simple model with 2 leaf states to describe the control of a ventilation fan. The fan turns on when the temperature is greater than 100 degrees; it turns off when the temperature is less than 80 degrees. The system checks the temperature periodically to determine whether to turn the fan on or off. The model is diagramed on the following page.

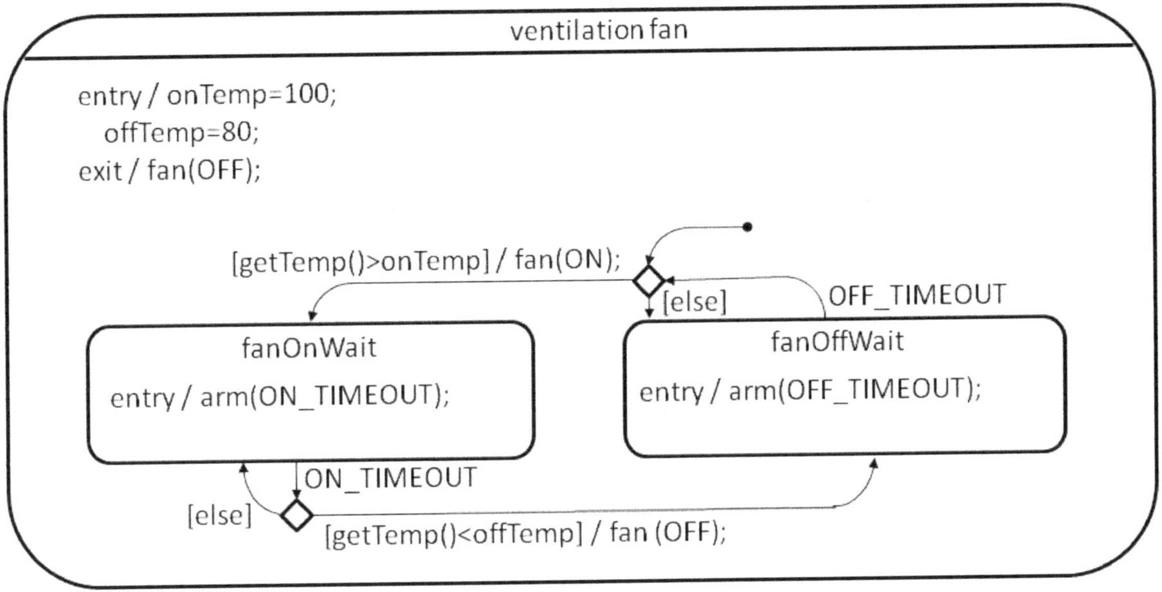
ventilation fan
entry / onTemp=100;
offTemp=80;
exit / fan(OFF);
[getTemp()>onTemp] / fan(ON);
[else]
OFF_TIMEOUT
fanOnWait
entry / arm(ON_TIMEOUT);
fanOffWait
entry / arm(OFF_TIMEOUT);
ON_TIMEOUT
[else]
[getTemp()<offTemp] / fan (OFF);

The test design uses 3 factors with values tabulated below.

Ventilation fan test factor values	
Factor	**Values**
getTemp()	70 79 80 90 100 101 110
from state	fanOffWait fanOnWait
trigger event	OFF_TIMEOUT[getTemp()<=onTemp]
	OFF_TIMEOUT[getTemp()>onTemp]
	ON_TIMEOUT[getTemp()<offTemp]
	ON_TIMEOUT[getTemp()>=offTemp]

State transitions are divided into 2 partitions, according to their expected target state. All pairs of values consistent with normal operation are included. Test cases for the first partition, transitions to the fanOffWait state, follow.

Transitions to fanOffWait		
getTemp()	**from state**	**trigger event**
70	fanOffWait	OFF_TIMEOUT[getTemp()<=onTemp]
70	fanOnWait	ON_TIMEOUT[getTemp()<offTemp]
79	fanOffWait	OFF_TIMEOUT[getTemp()<=onTemp]
80	fanOffWait	OFF_TIMEOUT[getTemp()<=onTemp]
90	fanOffWait	OFF_TIMEOUT[getTemp()<=onTemp]
100	fanOffWait	OFF_TIMEOUT[getTemp()<=onTemp]
79	fanOnWait	ON_TIMEOUT[getTemp()<offTemp]

Test cases for the second partition, transitions to the fanOnWait state, follow.

Transitions to fanOnWait		
getTemp()	**from state**	**trigger event**
101	fanOffWait	OFF_TIMEOUT[getTemp()>onTemp]
80	fanOnWait	ON_TIMEOUT[getTemp()>=offTemp]
110	fanOffWait	OFF_TIMEOUT[getTemp()>onTemp]
90	fanOnWait	ON_TIMEOUT[getTemp()>=offTemp]
100	fanOnWait	ON_TIMEOUT[getTemp()>=offTemp]
101	fanOnWait	ON_TIMEOUT[getTemp()>=offTemp]
110	fanOnWait	ON_TIMEOUT[getTemp()>=offTemp]

Stand-alone test models

When there is only one state model to test, a stand-alone test model is used. States of other regions (if present) are not test factors in these designs. We can choose one of 2 test models depending on the scope and goals of the test job. These are the transition model and the target state model. (The ventilation fan test design shown above uses the target state model.)

Transition model

The stand-alone transition model uses a partition for each transition in the state model. In the ventilation fan example there are 4 possible transitions between the 2 states, so there are 4 partitions. Each of the partitions is associated only with the from and to states of its transition. Thus, all the test factor pairs in the partition also are associated with the from and to states.

Target state model

The stand-alone target state model uses a partition for all the transitions to each state. In the ventilation fan example there are 2 partitions for the 2 states. All test factor pairs in the partition are associated with the expected target state.

Generally the transition model can be viewed as more thorough than the target state model because all allowed pairs are to be tested with the from state, as well as the to state. The transition model designs usually lead to additional test cases also.

Integrated test models

When there are multiple regions to test, an integrated test model may be used. States of other regions are used as test factors in these designs. As with the stand-alone models, these models test one region at a time, but the current states of other regions can be included as needed.

Integrated test models require the other regions' states to be as specified in the test case when the trigger event happens. Thus, the testability of the system is an important consideration in choosing one of the models. If the states of the other regions in the test cannot be controlled, use of these models may not be feasible.

Three integrated test models are briefly introduced here – the transition model, the target state model and the propagation model. Additional detail and examples are available at Testcover.com.

Transition model

The integrated transition model is the most comprehensive model for testing a single region, and it typically leads to the most test cases. Test factors include the current state and trigger event for the region under test, as well as relevant program variables. In the integrated transition model, the current states of other regions are included as test factors also. Each state transition in this region has one partition, and each partition has a test case covering every pair of other regions' states. Compared with the integrated target state model (below), the integrated transition model calls for additional testing of the effects other regions' states may have on this region.

Target state model

The integrated target state model includes the current states of the other regions, but it reduces the number of partitions to yield fewer test cases. The test factors are the same as those for the integrated transition model. The difference is that the integrated target state model defines a partition to include all the transitions leading to a particular target state. The integrated target state model only guarantees that all pairs of other regions' states are associated with the target state. However, using the current states of all regions as test factors assures that all pairs of current states leading to the target state are included in test cases.

Propagation model

The integrated propagation model differs from the other models in that its purpose is to test the effects of this region's transitions on other regions. The test factors are the same as those for the integrated target state model. It also defines a partition to include all the transitions leading to a particular target state. However, in this model, combinations of states, trigger events, and program variable values are selected to test only the positive consequences of this region's behavior on other regions. Generally, test factor values which do not cause observable interactions with other regions are excluded. Typically the number of test cases in the integrated propagation model is less than those of the other integrated test models.

Considerations for higher-strength designs

When we consider a complex system with **k** inputs, each of which can take one of **v** values, there are v^k possible input combinations. A question that sometimes arises is, "Instead of using a pairwise or 2-at-a-time test design, should we use a 3-at-a-time or 4-at-a-time design?" The goal is more complete test coverage of course. In theory we can have a strength-**t** or **t**-at-a-time design with any $t \leq k$. But whether higher-strength designs can improve the effectiveness of a test project depends on several considerations outlined in this section.

Number of test cases

The number of test cases for a higher-strength design increases rapidly with **t.** With a pairwise design there are on the order of v^2 test cases. A strength-**t** design needs about v^t test cases. Thus, for $v = 4$, a pairwise design of 16 test cases can be expected to increase to 64 or 256 cases for $t = 3$ or 4 respectively.

The increased number of test cases can affect a test project in a few different ways. Perhaps most important are the increases in schedule time and labor to execute the test cases and to analyze and document their results. There also are increases in time to generate the test cases because they require more computation. And if a change to the system requires regenerating test cases, the impact to the project may be larger than with pairwise designs.

On the other hand, additional test cases may result in more complete coverage, and additional faults may be discovered. We can expect diminishing returns here as the number of test cases is increased to find a fixed number of faults.

System behavior

One important issue that persists for higher-strength designs is that our system with **k** inputs has **s** states which respond to inputs differently. A sequence of inputs is needed to set up each initial state, and then a partition of test inputs is needed to obtain the expected result state. Simply selecting $\mathbf{v}^t$ test cases instead of $\mathbf{v}^2$ will test more combinations, but we still will not know what has been tested without considering system behavior. The partitioning techniques described in the earlier examples for input values and for state models can be applied to higher-strength designs also.

Combinations for set-up and partitioning

Frequently combinations of 3 or more test values are needed to set up a test case or to constrain a partition for an expected result. These larger combinations do *not* prove a need for a higher-strength test design. For example, to test the normal operation of a calendar application, a partition may contain combinations of month, day and year. The selection of the values must reflect the correct operation of the system. Whether the test design is pairwise or 3-at-a-time is an independent consideration.

The following calendar example illustrates a pairwise design in which the partition is constrained by combinations of 3 variables.

Calendar example test factor values	
Factor	**Values**
Month	jan feb mar apr may jun jul aug sep oct nov dec
Day	1 10 28 29 30 31
Year	2012 2013

For this normal operation partition, each month is tested with its first day, 10th day and last day, and with a leap year and a common year. The following test cases include all allowed pairs of values, constrained by the usual calendar rules.

Calendar example dates					
Month	**Day**	**Year**	**Month**	**Day**	**Year**
jan	1	2012	oct	10	2013
feb	10	2012	nov	1	2013
feb	1	2013	nov	10	2012
jan	10	2013	dec	1	2012
mar	31	2013	dec	10	2013
may	31	2012	feb	28	2013
apr	30	2012	feb	29	2012
jun	30	2013	mar	1	2013
mar	10	2012	apr	1	2012
apr	10	2013	may	10	2012
may	1	2013	jun	10	2013
jun	1	2012	jan	31	2012
jul	1	2013	jul	31	2012
jul	10	2012	aug	31	2012
aug	1	2012	oct	31	2012
aug	10	2013	dec	31	2012
sep	1	2013	sep	30	2012
sep	10	2012	nov	30	2012
oct	1	2012			

In this example if the date "feb 29 2012" fails for incorrect treatment of the leap year, it does not logically follow that a higher-strength design is required to find the fault: The case is covered in this pairwise design.

In summary, a higher-strength design may discover additional faults with a cost of an exponential increase in test cases. As with pairwise designs, it is important not to overlook the existence of multiple states and the need to set them up for testing. Use of larger combinations of input values is not a substitute for test cases designed to exercise required system behavior. Finally, it is important not to conflate the number of factors required for set-up and partition constraints with a need for a higher-strength design.

Considerations for tool selection

This section outlines considerations for the selection of a pairwise design tool. These include:

- number of test cases
- response time
- constraint handling and ease of use
- integration with other tools

Generally an evaluation of a candidate tool by the development organization is recommended. Experience applying the tool to typical test design situations can be a valuable way to identify issues and benefits.

Number of test cases

The number of test cases is an essential consideration because the time and cost of a test project depend strongly on how much testing is to be done. Compared with random selection, pairwise designs require far fewer test cases for comparable coverage. Nevertheless, different pairwise tools generate different numbers of test cases. The Available Tools page at Pairwise.org compares the numbers of test cases generated by various tools for a few examples.

Generally the number of test cases and the time to generate them increase with the number of test factors and their values. The fewest number of test cases possible is the product $\mathbf{v_1}$ x $\mathbf{v_2}$, in which $\mathbf{v_1}$ and $\mathbf{v_2}$ are the numbers of values of the 2 largest factors. (This is the number of pairs for these 2 factors alone.) As the number of factors is increased, the minimum number of test cases increases from $\mathbf{v_1}$ x $\mathbf{v_2}$ slowly.

Response time

The overall performance of a pairwise test case generator depends on two essential components: the number of test cases produced and the response time for generating them. Practical software engineering tools require an optimal balance between the two. A quick response with many test cases may present the test team with unnecessary work. On the other hand, a fast-paced development organization needs tools that can keep up.

Obviously pairwise tools that give prompt responses save time. Beyond that, having faster, easy-to-use tools can improve test plans. It should be quick and simple to answer questions like:

- What if we add a test factor?
- What if we change the number of values?

If the tool makes it easier to accommodate the inevitable late changes to the test plan, everybody benefits.

Constraint handling

From the earlier examples it is clear that practical pairwise design tools must accommodate the constraints found in real systems. They must be able to include or exclude complex combinations without dropping required pairs.

The means to specify the constraints varies among different tools. Some use rules to define constraints explicitly. Others use implicit methods to designate which combinations are allowed. Both approaches can work in principle. Including designs with constraints in evaluations of candidate tools is a good way to clarify their differences. These differences may indicate preferences in efficiency of defining constraints, ease of use, etc.

Integration with other tools

Pairwise test tools have been designed with many different interfaces. These range from command line interfaces to GUIs, HTML and XML. Some tools provide more than one interface.

It is important to consider development tools and processes in selecting a pairwise tool. Relevant questions include:

- How do the pairwise designs fit with current tools, for test automation, test management and system modeling?
- What development process and tool changes are anticipated in the future?
- Does the pairwise tool support integration with other tools for increased efficiency and process improvements?

These considerations will help to get the most from pairwise testing.

Direct Product Block notation

This appendix contains the input data used for the pairwise design examples in this guide. Interested readers can reproduce the test cases by submitting the requests into the Testcover.com test case generator form.

The requests use Direct Product Block (DPB) notation to specify test factor values and their constraints. Generally allowed values for a factor appear on the same line. Multiple lines following the plus (+) character indicate allowed combinations of values in a block. One or more blocks following the pound (#) character define the allowed combinations in a partition. The complete DPB specification is available to subscribers at Testcover.com.

Configurations without constraints

This request generates the networked computer configurations without constraints. They are equivalent to the configurations given by the orthogonal array template.

```
Configurations without constraints
Op system
Connection
Browser
Application
#
+
XP Vista Win7
wi-fi dsl cable
IE Firefox Safari
App1 App2 App3
```

Configurations with constraints

This request generates the networked computer configurations with constraints. It is not possible to use an orthogonal array template here because of the constraints restricting browser and operating system combinations.

```
Configurations with constraints
Op system
Connection
Browser
Application
#
+ (XP MacOS Linux) with Firefox
XP MacOS Linux
wi-fi dsl cable
Firefox
App1 App2 App3
+ (XP MacOS) with Safari
XP MacOS
wi-fi dsl cable
Safari
App1 App2 App3
+ XP with IE
XP
wi-fi dsl cable
IE
App1 App2 App3
```

Design-your-burger form inputs

This request generates the design-your-burger form inputs. Inputs from the reset button and links on the form were excluded from the partition to test the action of the submit button and verify its expected results.

```
Design-your-burger form inputs
Burger
Cooked
Cheese
Lettuce
Tomato
Onion
Ketchup
Mustard
Mayo
Secret sauce
#
beef turkey veggie
none rare medium well
no yes
no yes
no yes
no yes
no yes
no yes
no yes
no yes
```

Reservation database records

This request generates the motel reservation database table records. The 3 blocks for the single room, standard room and suite contain the allowed combinations of values according to the motel's business rules. The single value room_ID is a placeholder to be replaced with a unique identifier in each record.

```
Reservation database records
Location ID
Room ID
Room type
Section
Smoking
Beds
Convertible couch
Near gym/spa
Near business center
Wi-fi
Phone lines
Balcony/patio
#
+ single room
location_1 location_2 location_3
room_ID
single
floor_1 tower
no yes
single
no
no
no
no
1
no
+ standard room
location_1 location_2 location_3
room_ID
standard
floor_1 mezzanine tower
```

```
no yes
2_queen 1_king
no
no yes
no yes
no yes
1
no yes
+ suite
location_1 location_2 location_3
room_ID
suite
mezzanine tower
no yes
2_queen
yes
yes
yes
yes
2
yes
```

Ventilation fan transition design

This request generates the stand-alone transition design for the ventilation fan state model. The 4 partitions correspond to the transitions among the 2 leaf states.

```
Ventilation fan transition design
getTemp()
from state
event
# fanOffWait to fanOffWait
70 79 80 90 100
fanOffWait
OFF_TIMEOUT[getTemp()<=onTemp]
# fanOnWait to fanOffWait
70 79
fanOnWait
ON_TIMEOUT[getTemp()<offTemp]
# fanOffWait to fanOnWait
101 110
fanOffWait
OFF_TIMEOUT[getTemp()>onTemp]
# fanOnWait to fanOnWait
80 90 100 101 110
fanOnWait
ON_TIMEOUT[getTemp()>=offTemp]
```

Ventilation fan target state design

This request generates the stand-alone target state design for the ventilation fan state model. The 2 partitions include all the transitions to each of the 2 states.

The blocks in the 2 ventilation fan test designs are the same, but they are partitioned differently. Often the target state model yields fewer test cases than the corresponding transition model. In this very simple example, the same 14 test cases (shown earlier) are generated by both models. The test cases are just partitioned differently.

```
Ventilation fan target state design
getTemp()
from state
event
# Transitions to fanOffWait
+ fanOffWait to fanOffWait
70 79 80 90 100
fanOffWait
OFF_TIMEOUT[getTemp()<=onTemp]
+ fanOnWait to fanOffWait
70 79
fanOnWait
ON_TIMEOUT[getTemp()<offTemp]
# Transitions to fanOnWait
+ fanOffWait to fanOnWait
101 110
fanOffWait
OFF_TIMEOUT[getTemp()>onTemp]
+ fanOnWait to fanOnWait
80 90 100 101 110
fanOnWait
ON_TIMEOUT[getTemp()>=offTemp]
```

Calendar example dates

This request generates the dates for the calendar example. There is one partition comprised of 5 blocks as follows.

- **the first and 10th day of each month**
- **the last day of months with 31 days**
- **the last day of months with 30 days**
- **the last day of February in a common year**
- **the last day of February in a leap year**

```
Calendar Example
Month
Day
Year
#ok All good dates
jan feb mar apr may jun jul aug sep oct nov dec
1 10
2012 2013
+ long month last day
jan mar may jul aug oct dec
31
2012 2013
+ short month last day
apr jun sep nov
30
2012 2013
+ feb last day
feb
28
2013
+ leap day
feb
29
2012
```

About the author

George Sherwood is the inventor of CATS, the first pairwise test tool to use a greedy search to handle test system constraints. He worked for 25 years at Bell Labs and AT&T Labs on a variety of hardware, software and service development projects. He has managed teams of engineers on work ranging from system engineering and project management to system testing and field support.

In 2003 George founded Testcover.com to enable software engineers to design more effective test plans with fewer test cases. He has found innovative constructions for covering arrays (test templates) which are described in the *Journal of Combinatorial Designs* and *Discrete Mathematics*. At Testcover.com he also devised significant improvements to search algorithms. This work has led to pairwise designs with fewer test cases and quicker results.

About Testcover.com

Testcover.com offers a pairwise test case generator that helps testers get the results they need to develop optimal products and services in a fraction of the time, saving time and money on every project. Testcover.com is accessible via the cloud – a software as a service (SaaS) independent test design solution – and its Web Services Description Language (WSDL) interface enables ready integration with existing test tools.

www.ingramcontent.com/pod-product-compliance
Lightning Source LLC
Chambersburg PA
CBHW060933050326
40689CB00013B/3069
* 9 7 8 1 4 6 8 0 1 0 3 3 6 *